The Cat in the Hat's Learning Library

P9-BBU-949

To Johnny and Melody, with love.
—T.R.

The editors would like to thank
BARBARA KIEFER, Ph.D.,
Charlotte S. Huck Professor of Children's Literature,
The Ohio State University, and
JOSEPH M. MORAN, Ph.D.,
Associate Director of Education,
American Meteorological Society,
for their assistance in the preparation of this book.

TM & copyright © by Dr. Seuss Enterprises, L.P. 2004
THE CAT IN THE HAT'S LEARNING LIBRARY logos and word mark are registered trademarks of
Dr. Seuss Enterprises, L.P.
THE CAT IN THE HAT'S LEARNING LIBRARY logos © Dr. Seuss Enterprises, L.P. 1998

All rights reserved. Published in the United States by Random House Children's Books,
a division of Random House, Inc., New York.

Random House and the colophon are registered trademarks of Random House, Inc.

Visit us on the Web!
www.randomhouse.com/kids
Seussville.com

Educators and librarians, for a variety of teaching tools, visit us at
www.randomhouse.com/teachers

Library of Congress Cataloging-in-Publication Data
Rabe, Tish.
Oh say can you say what's the weather today? : all about weather / by Tish Rabe ; illustrated by
Aristides Ruiz.
   p. cm. — (The Cat in the Hat's learning library)
Summary: In rhyming text, the Cat in the Hat teaches Sally and Dick about different weather
conditions and how we learn about them.
ISBN 978-0-375-82276-6 (trade) — ISBN 978-0-375-92276-3 (lib. bdg.)
1. Weather—Juvenile literature. [1. Weather.] I. Ruiz, Aristides, ill. II. Title. III. Series.
QC981.3.R33 2004 551.6—dc21 2003004683

Printed in the United States of America
27 26 25 24 23 22 21

Random House Children's Books supports the First Amendment and celebrates the right to read.

Oh Say Can You Say What's the Weather Today?

by Tish Rabe

illustrated by Aristides Ruiz

The Cat in the Hat's Learning Library®

Random House New York

I'm the Cat in the Hat
and it's raining, I know,
but let's not stay inside—
we've got places to go!

Where the sunshine is shining,
where warm winds are blowing,
where lightning is flashing,
where snowflakes are snowing.

The weather is changing.
Come on! Let's get going!

First stop is the top
of Mount Karakakoo,
where they study the weather.
(That's all that they do!)

Watching the weather
helps everyone know
what to wear, where to live,
and what food they can grow.

Pilots check weather
when they fly a plane.
Are they flying in sunshine
or clouds filled with rain?

Corn grows where it's hot.
Rice grows where it's wet.

Farmers grow what grows best
in the weather they get.

Meteorologists forecast
the weather and say
what kind of weather
is heading our way.

They send weather balloons
floating high in the air
to measure how hot
or how cold it is there.

Air temperature
affects weather a lot.
Thermometers show
if it's cold or it's hot.

10

Wind changes weather
and we can see why.
It blows clouds along
and clears rain from the sky.

An–e–mom–e–ters measure
how fast the wind goes.
A wind vane will show you
which way the wind blows.

11

On this map of the weather
you'll see it is showing
it's sunny in Gret,
but in Groogle it's snowing.

GROOGLE

A strong wind is blowing
the snow right toward Gret.
Tomorrow the weather
in Gret will be wet.

Symbols on weather maps
show right away
what kind of weather
we're having today.

GRET

THIS SYMBOL 9❜9 means drizzle, and this one ●● means rain.
✳ ✳ This means it's snowing.
This means ❜ HURRICANE!

Weather forecasts
are important to us.
Will we need a jacket
to wait for the bus?

When clouds form a ring
and it circles the moon,
sailors know this ring means
there's a storm coming soon.

A pine cone can forecast
the weather. Here's why.
It's closed when it's wet.
Opened up when it's dry.

Here is a fact that
we cannot explain.
Frogs croak a lot more
when it's going to rain.

CROAK!

CROAK!

CROAK!

CROAK!

There are all kinds of clouds
you can see in the sky.
Cirrus are light, wispy
clouds floating by.

CIRRUS

CUMULONIMBUS

CUMULUS

Cumulonimbus clouds mean
there's a storm on the way.
You see cumulus clouds
on a warm, sunny day.

16

When a cloud touches down
on the ground, it's called fog.
If it mixes with smoke,
then the fog becomes smog.

SMOG

SMOG

SMOG

FOG

A fun way to learn a
cloud's shape is to draw it.
We said, "That's a cirrus!"
the minute we saw it.

17

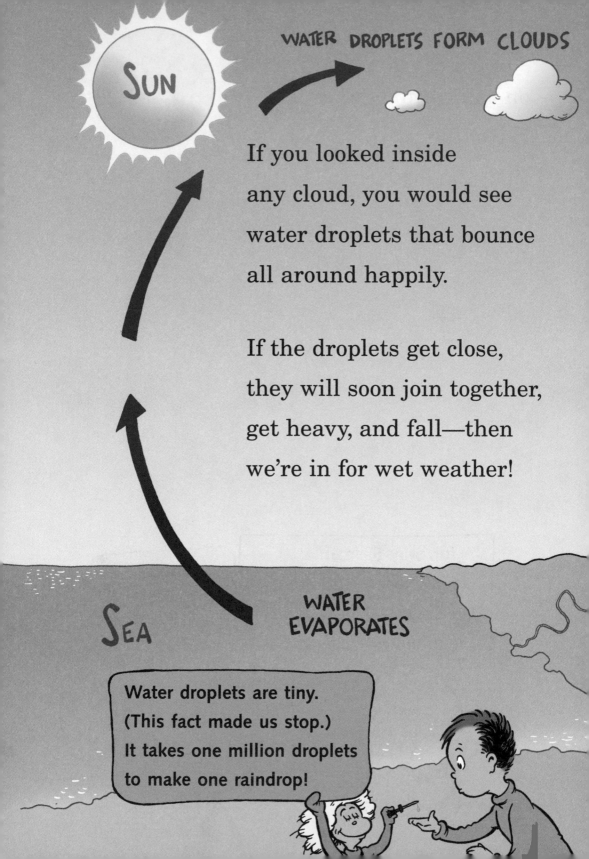

SUN

WATER DROPLETS FORM CLOUDS

If you looked inside
any cloud, you would see
water droplets that bounce
all around happily.

If the droplets get close,
they will soon join together,
get heavy, and fall—then
we're in for wet weather!

SEA

WATER
EVAPORATES

Water droplets are tiny.
(This fact made us stop.)
It takes one million droplets
to make one raindrop!

They fall to the ground,
then the sun's energy
turns them to water vapor,
which we cannot see.

Water vapor floats up,
forms a new cloud, and then
rain falls from the cloud
to the ground once again.

RAIN

RIVER

LAKE

RUN OFF

Guess what they call this.
(Give it a trycle!)
The path of the rain is
called the water cycle!

19

Here are some words that we learned on vacation. Rain, snow, sleet, and hail are called precipitation.

Water changing to vapor
is called evaporation.

Vapor changing to water
is called condensation.

Who invented umbrellas?

Well, we don't know who . . .
but umbrellas were first
made in China. It's true!
Out of colorful paper
and wood called bamboo.

Thousands of years ago
they were first made,
so out in the sun
folks could walk in the shade.

When it rained, they put
wax on the paper. Here's why.
Rain rolled off the wax,
which kept folks nice and dry.

When air's warmer than freezing
I'd like to explain,
water falls from the clouds
and it falls down as rain.

When air's freezing cold,
it's important to know,
water falls from the clouds,
but it falls down as snow.

The desert is dry
and the reason is clear.
Its rainfall is less
than ten inches a year.

Here is a word and we
both like to rhyme it.
The weather a place has
the most is its climate.

How do you keep cool
when you live in a land
that is hot, dry, and dusty
and covered in sand?

Loose-fitting clothes
let breezes blow through,
and light colors bounce
the sun's rays off you.

27

Where on earth is it coldest?
Meteorologists say
Antarctica is
freezing cold every day.

Land covered in ice
and deep, drifting snow.
The air is so cold
that plants cannot grow.

28

In a tropical jungle
it's hot and it's wet.
If you go there to visit,
you soon start to sweat.

The weather is humid,
which makes you feel icky.
The air's full of water.
That's why you feel sticky.

Air conditioners help you
feel better. Here's why.
Cold air holds less water—
so you feel cool and dry.

In a thunderstorm first
you will see lightning flash!
Next you'll hear thunder
go rumble and crash!

To find out how far
thunderstorms are from you,
try this easy trick.
It's a fun thing to do.

Start counting when you
see a lightning bolt flash.
Stop counting when you hear
the next thunder crash.

20

...18
...19
...20!

Take that number, divide it by five. When you do, that's the number of miles that the storm is from you!

Lightning's electric! One flash is so strong it could light every light in your house all year long.

Thunder won't hurt you,
but lightning could, so . . .
here are a few things
we would like you to know.

Lightning strikes what is tallest,
so take it from me—
in a thunderstorm NEVER
stand under a tree!

If you're out in a field and have no place to go, get as small as you can and then scrunch way down low.

Stay inside your car.
If there's lightning around,
it flows over your car
and down into the ground.

35

If strong winds are blowing
with hard, driving rain,
you may be in the middle
of a HURRICANE!

Winds blow in a circle
both night and day,
knocking lots of things down
that get in their way.

Here's a hurricane fact that's a favorite of mine. There can be lots of hurricanes at the same time.

So each one gets a name—Andrew, Agnes, or Dora, Lenny, Dianna, Mitch, Bertha, or Flora.

They each get a name so there's never a doubt which hurricane people are talking about.

DORA

FLORA

37

Hurricanes blow things down,
but I learned from Thing Two,
tornadoes blow harder
than hurricanes do!

A tornado picks up
everything it goes by,
like a huge vacuum cleaner
way up in the sky.

It spins like a top,
twirling round and around,
pulling trees, cars, and houses
right off of the ground!

Once in a tornado
a chicken was tossed.
She landed safely,
but her feathers were lost!

It's important to study
the weather! It's true.
But we cannot control it,
whatever we do.

The sun may be shining,
the sky a bright blue.
Then suddenly rain
will start falling on you.

Or the sky may be filled with
dark storm clouds and then
the sun will break through
and shine down once again.

You see, weather keeps changing,
but one thing we know.
It makes life exciting
wherever you go.

GLOSSARY

Anemometer: An instrument that measures the speed of the wind.

Cirrus: Clouds that look like feathery, wispy streaks in the sky.

Condensation: Changing from a gas to a liquid.

Crystals: Solid pieces of material that have a regular pattern of flat surfaces and angles.

Cumulus: Fluffy white clouds that can appear on a warm, sunny day.

Evaporation: Changing from a liquid to a gas.

Forecast: A prediction of what will likely happen in the future.

Hail: Pieces of ice that fall from a thunderstorm cloud like rain.

Humid: Damp, slightly wet.

Magnify: To make something look bigger than its true size.

Meteorologist: A scientist who studies the earth's weather.

Nimbostratus: Thick, low gray clouds that cover the sky, block out the sun, and produce rain or snow.

Precipitation: Water that falls to the ground as rain, snow, sleet, or hail.

Sleet: Frozen raindrops.

Smog: A mixture of polluted air, smoke, or fog.

Stratus: Low gray clouds that form in layers and sometimes produce drizzle.

Temperature: The measure of how cold or hot something is.

Thermometer: A glass tube filled with alcohol that rises and falls as the temperature of the air around it goes up and down; an electronic or digital instrument that measures temperature.

FOR FURTHER READING

The Cloud Book by Tomie de Paola (Holiday House).
Discover more about clouds in this fun book. For
preschoolers and up.

Flash, Crash, Rumble, and Roll by Franklyn M.
Branley, illustrated by True Kelley (HarperCollins,
Let's-Read-and-Find-Out Science). Learn all about
those scary storm noises! For kindergarten and up.

Twisters and Other Terrible Storms by Will Osborne
and Mary Pope Osborne (Random House, *Magic Tree
House Research Guide*). Find out the answers to
questions about nature's wildest weather. For grades
2 and up.

Weather by Seymour Simon (HarperTrophy).
Beautiful photographs combined with great weather
information. For kindergarten and up.

Weather Words and What They Mean by Gail
Gibbons (Holiday House). Learn more about the
weather words you just discovered! For kindergarten
and up.

INDEX

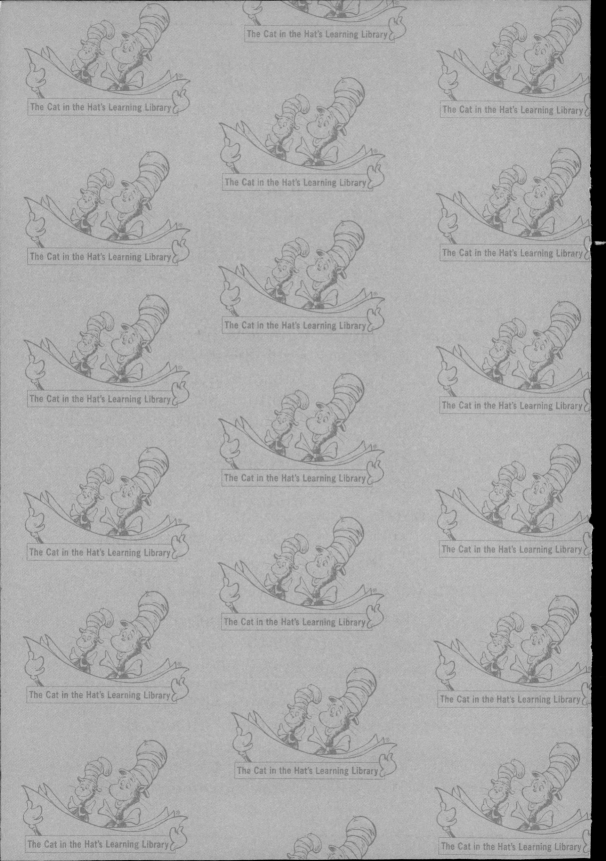